Employment Tribunal Compensation

By Daniel Barnett

The Employment Law Library

All books in the Employment Law Library are sent for free to members of the HR Inner Circle.

1. Employee Investigations
2. GDPR for HR Professionals
3. Preventing and Defending Employee Stress Claims
4. Employment Tribunal Time Limits
5. Deconstructing TUPE
6. Changing Terms & Conditions
7. Constructive Dismissal
8. Resolving Grievances
9. HR Hazards
10. Employment Status
11. Spotting Malingering
12. Employment Tribunal Compensation
13. Hiring Staff

Published by Employment Law Services Limited, Unit 3, Chequers Farm, Chequers Lane, Watford, Hertfordshire WD25 0LG

ISBN 978-1-913925-06-2

EMPLOYMENT
LAW
MATTERS

Subscribe to
Daniel Barnett's podcast

EMPLOYMENT LAW MATTERS

via iTunes, Spotify, or your
favourite podcast player

WWW.DANIELBARNETT.CO.UK/PODCAST

Acknowledgments

This is the twelfth book in my series of mini guides on employment law for HR professionals.

As always, there are a number of people to thank. First and foremost, I'd like to thank Becky Renauta for her help with the content. I'd also like to thank Tincuta Moscaliuc for the layout and design, Aaron Gaff for proofreading and Maria Rodriguez for converting the book into the formats needed for Amazon.

I'd also like to thank the members of the HR Inner Circle for whom I primarily write these small books (and who get them all for free as part of their membership). In particular, I'd like to thank several members who looked at an early manuscript and made suggestions to improve it, namely, Penelope Douglass, Emma Vernon, Mandy Fitzmaurice, Claire Thompson and Patrick McNamee. If you're interested in learning more about HR Inner Circle membership (www. hrinnercircle.co.uk), there is more information at the back of this book.

Daniel Barnett
May 2022

ABOUT THE AUTHOR

Daniel Barnett is a leading employment law barrister practising from Outer Temple Chambers. With 25 years' experience defending public and private sector employers against employment claims, he has represented a Royal Family, several international airlines, FTSE-100 companies and various NHS Trusts and local authorities. Employee clients include David & Victoria Beckham's nanny and Paul Mason (subject of the ITV documentary 'Britain's Fattest Man').

Daniel is a past chair of the Employment Lawyers' Association's publishing committee and electronic services working party. He is the author or co-author of eight books, including the Law Society Handbook on Employment Law (currently in its 8th edition). He is the creator of the Employment Law (UK) mailing list, an email alerter bulletin service sending details of breaking news in employment law three times a week to 33,000 recipients.

Legal directories describe him as 'extremely knowledgeable and [he] can absorb pages of instructions at lightning speed', 'involved in a number of highly contentious matters', 'singled out for his work for large blue-chip companies', 'combination of in-depth legal knowledge, pragmatism, quick response times and approachability', 'inexhaustible', 'tenacious', 'knowledgeable', and 'an excellent advocate'.

He is one of the leading speakers and trainers on the employment law and HR circuit. He has presented seminars for the House of Commons, the BBC, Oxford University, HSBC, Barclays Bank, Ocado, and dozens of other organisations in-house. In 2013, 2014, 2016, and 2019 he designed — and was the sole speaker at — the Employment Law MasterClass national tour.

As well as full-time practice as a barrister and speaker, Daniel is the founder of the HR Inner Circle – a membership club for smart, ambitious HR Professionals. In 2007, he co-founded CPD Webinars Ltd, then the UK's leading webinar training company for lawyers, and sold it to Thomson Reuters in 2011.

Daniel is widely sought after as a commentator in both broadcast and print media on all legal issues. Since 2010 he has presented the Legal Hour on LBC Radio. In 2019, he launched Employment Law Matters, a weekly podcast with short explanations of employment law topics. Subscribe at www.danielbarnett.co.uk/podcast

www.danielbarnett.co.uk
Temple, London

Contents

All employment and HR practitioners are competing for work in a market where clients are more conscious of spend, and competitors from ABSs & large independent consultancies encroach into the market.

In Intelligent Marketing for Employment Lawyers you will discover how the internet can revolutionise the way you do business and generate new clients, as well as increasing fees and obtaining more work from existing clients.

Visit
GO.DANIELBARNETT.COM/BOOKS
for more information.

Introduction

If an employee (known as the 'Claimant') wins an employment tribunal claim, there will be a 'remedy hearing' to assess how much money (or 'compensation') they should be awarded.

In this book, you'll learn how this compensation is assessed by tribunals and what employers (or by this stage 'Respondents') can do to limit the award.

However, that is not to say that the information in this book is only relevant at the final remedy stage. In fact, thinking about an employee's potential compensation early on is a very useful case management technique. It can focus both parties' minds on the hard facts of what a claim is actually worth. If that leads to settlement or, even better, withdrawal of the claim, that has to be worth the time spent on early planning.

Fortunately, in most circumstances, valuing the employee's financial loss is reasonably straightforward. There is a standard approach to calculating the various parts, for which this book provides an overview. However, I also delve a bit deeper into the trickier issues and give handy hints for dealing with them.

CHAPTER 1:
Introduction to unfair dismissal compensation

Compensation for unfair dismissal is split into two parts: the 'basic award' and the 'compensatory award'.

Basic award

The 'basic award' is straightforward. It is calculated using a mathematical formula set out in the *Employment Rights Act (ERA) 1996*, which is very similar to the calculation used for statutory redundancy payments.

The calculation involves multiplying the employee's number of full years' continuous employment by a week's pay, adjusted according to their age.

For each year of employment under the age of 22, the employee will receive half a week's pay; between ages 22 and 41, they'll receive one week's pay; and for each year of employment after 41, they'll receive one and a half weeks' pay.

A week's pay is generally the employee's gross standard weekly wage at the end of their employment (or average wage over the 12 weeks prior to the employment termination date if the employee's pay varies from week to week). A week's pay is currently capped at £571 (as of May 2022), and this increases by the rate of inflation on 6 April every year.

The maximum basic award would be for an employee who, at the time of dismissal had 20 or more years' continuous service, during no part of which they were under 41 years old, and who earned gross pay of at least £571 per week. The employee would be entitled to a basic award of 20 years x 1½ weeks' pay for each year x maximum week's pay of £571 = £17,1

Example calculation of the basic award

Taj is 50 years old at the end of his employment. He has been continuously employed for 19 years (only counting full years of service) since he was 31 years old. His weekly pay before tax and any other deductions is £500.

Step 1: 1 week's pay x 10 years of service under 41 = 10 weeks' pay

Step 2: 1.5 weeks' pay x 9 years of service over 41 = 13.5 weeks' pay

Step 3: 10 weeks + 13.5 weeks = 23.5 weeks' pay.

Step 4: £500 weekly pay x 23.5 weeks = £11,750

Compensatory award

The compensatory award is trickier to calculate. It is harder to predict with any great accuracy what an employment tribunal may award. This is unfortunate as it is usually the larger part of unfair dismissal compensation.

It not only involves calculating the employee's current financial loss but also any financial losses in the future. The vague nature of the compensatory award is reflected in its vague definition in section 123 of the *ERA 1996*, namely:

> *"such amount as the tribunal considers just and equitable in all the circumstances having regard to the loss sustained by the complainant in consequence of the dismissal, insofar as that loss is attributable to action taken by the employer."*

The award is based on the employee's net loss of earnings, including benefits and pension contributions where relevant (contrast that with the basic award, which is based on gross weekly earnings).

The amount payable may be reduced when an employee fails to take reasonable action to 'mitigate' or reduce their loss by finding alternative work, or where their inappropriate behaviour has contributed to their dismissal. The loss can also be increased or decreased by up to 25% where the employer or employee has unreasonably failed to follow the *Acas Code of Practice on Disciplinary and Grievance Procedures.*

Helpfully, to make it all a bit easier (or at least cheaper), there is normally a cap on the amount of compensation that a tribunal can order to be paid. This is currently set at the lower figure of:

- one year's gross pay

- £93,878 (as of 6 April 2022 – it increases by the rate of inflation on 6 April every year).

The cap does not apply in cases where the reason for the dismissal was related to discrimination, whistleblowing, pregnancy or health and safety – meaning compensation is, at least in theory, unlimited (but always based on financial losses, so lower earners will not recover as much as higher earners). I'll come back to how and when this cap is applied in Chapter 6.

Unlike discrimination awards, a tribunal will not award any compensation for 'injury to feelings' in unfair dismissal cases. Additionally, unlike discrimination awards, a tribunal cannot award interest on an unfair dismissal award.

CHAPTER 2
Introduction to discrimination compensation

Compensation for discrimination is normally made up of two parts: financial loss and injury to feelings. However, tribunals can also award other types of compensation (personal injury, aggravated damages) in certain situations.

An injury to feelings award provides an employee with compensation for the hurt and upset caused by discriminatory conduct. This award is unrelated to financial loss. I'll come back to look at this type of award in more detail in Chapter 5.

Financial loss is usually the employee's loss of earnings arising from the discriminatory act. The purpose of the award is to put the employee in the position that they would have been in if the discrimination had not happened. This loss of earnings could be the result of being dismissed (or resigning because of, say, sexual harassment), but could also include loss incurred from discrimination such as a failure to award a promotion, pay rise, bonus or commission payments. These payments would be included in any sum for loss of earnings, as well as basic salary.

If the discrimination results in the end of the employment, then (like unfair dismissal compensation) the tribunal will need to calculate past and future losses. While the principles of assessing this compensation are similar, there are differences worth knowing about. The concepts of 'basic' and 'compensatory' awards do not exist in discrimination cases. More significantly, there is no cap on the limit of the award for financial loss.

Another distinction between unfair dismissal and discrimination compensation is that it is not only the employer that is at risk of an award being made against it. In discrimination claims, tribunals can order that the award is made against any person who actually committed the acts of discrimination. This can be a manager or another member of the employer's staff. In discrimination cases, tribunals also tend to be more sympathetic to the employee's assertions that they will have difficulty obtaining further employment.

In addition, tribunals have the power to order interest on compensation awards for discrimination. This is fixed by the *Judgments Act 1838* and is currently 8%. Interest accrues daily from the date of the first act of discrimination for injury to feelings awards, or from the mid-point between the first act of discrimination and the date of calculation of the damages for other compensation.

Given these advantages to employees, where an employer is found liable for both unfair dismissal and discrimination, in most cases, the tribunal will award the compensation under the discrimination head. In any event, whichever head of claim the tribunal chooses, the bulk of the award is normally for loss of earnings (unless the employee didn't suffer any financial loss or found a new job very quickly).

CHAPTER 3:
Calculating loss of earnings

The approach to calculating loss of earnings is the same in both unfair dismissal and discrimination claims (although the cap of a year's gross pay, or £93,878 if lower, applies in unfair dismissal claims).

The aim is to compensate the employee for all lost earnings they might reasonably be expected to have received but for the dismissal (this includes constructive dismissal – see Book 7 of the Employment Law Library).

This first involves establishing the employee's net (not gross) salary and factoring in the value of any benefits or pay rises they would have received. The benefits should not only include those to which the employee was entitled under their contract but also those the employee could reasonably expect to receive. Such benefits might include, for example, bonuses, commission, regular overtime or tips. Additional loss, such as pension rights or expenses associated with seeking new employment, can also be recovered.

Past loss

A tribunal will usually start its calculation by working out the employee's past loss of earnings. This is generally from the date of dismissal to the date of the remedy hearing (or, more accurately, to the date of the remedy judgment being sent out if the judgment is 'reserved' – which means not announced on the day and sent out in the post).

It is usually up to the employee to provide evidence of their financial losses by providing copies of their payslips (although the employer will be ordered to produce copies if the employee has not kept them).

It is also up to the employee to provide evidence that they have taken steps to reduce or 'mitigate' their losses, for example, by producing evidence of job applications. Mitigation is examined in detail in the next chapter.

Employers are also expected to (and will want to) provide any evidence to counter the (usually high) level of loss that the employee is asking for. Also, when the dismissal was only unfair due to flaws in the procedure, the compensation should be limited to the earnings the employee would have received if the correct procedure had been followed. This is commonly referred to as the '*Polkey*' principle, and it is taken from the decision in *Polkey v A E Dayton Services [1987] IRLR 503*. Again, *Polkey* is considered in detail in the next chapter.

Future loss

Once the tribunal has calculated the employee's past loss, it should then consider whether there will be any ongoing future loss (occurring after the date of the tribunal hearing).

If the employee has already found a new job on similar (or better) terms, any compensation they receive for future loss will be relatively small. However, if the employee has not yet got another job, or is now earning a lower salary, then the future loss may be more substantial. When assessing future loss, tribunals will consider issues such as the local job market and the factors relevant to the employee's circumstances, such as their age or childcare commitments.

Example calculation of loss of earnings

Samantha earns £400 net (after tax) per week with Employer A. She is dismissed by Employer A on 1 March and brings a tribunal claim for unfair dismissal. She starts a job with Employer B on 12 April, earning £350 per week. The tribunal hearing is on 3 May and the tribunal decides Samantha was unfairly dismissed.

Past loss: the tribunal awards £2,400 loss of earnings for the six-week period from 1 March to 12 April when Samantha was out of work (£400 x

6 weeks). It awards £150 for the three-week period from 12 April to 3 May when Samantha earned £50 less per week from Employer B than she would have received from Employer A.

Future loss: the tribunal agrees with Samantha that she is unlikely to be able to earn the same level of salary she was earning with Employer A for another 24 weeks. This is because:

- the local job market is not strong.

- she is limited in the jobs she can apply for as she needs to work school hours due to childcare commitments (she was working these hours with Employer A).

- she is unlikely to get a salary increase from Employer B until the end of the 24-week period.

The tribunal awards future loss of £1,200 (£50 weekly loss x 24 weeks). Samantha's total loss is £3,600 (£2,400 + £1,200).

Statutory cap

Where the statutory cap applies (in most unfair dismissal claims), the amount of the employee's ongoing loss is not so important. This is because it will be limited to the lower of the maximum statutory cap

– currently £93,878 for dismissals occurring on or after 6 April 2022 – or 12 months' gross salary. The statutory cap increases annually on 6 April.

However, it becomes really key in whistleblowing or discriminatory dismissals where there is no cap on the award. It is here that it can all add up to a very large sum – particularly if there are reasons why an employee will find it difficult to find another job, such as psychological problems caused by the discrimination.

Ogden Tables

It all gets tricky to calculate – so tricky that sometimes the tribunal might even refer to the government's 'Actuarial Tables for use in Personal Injury and Fatal Accident cases', otherwise known as the 'Ogden Tables'. These tables calculate lump sum compensation through the use of 'multipliers'. These account for factors such as likely future inflation, interest rates and life expectancy. On the whole, tribunals avoid using these tables in employment-related cases because they are primarily designed for personal injury cases. The two exceptions to this are calculating pension loss and career-long loss.

Career-long loss

On some (thankfully rare) occasions, it may be established that the employee is unlikely to get another job, or a job with equivalent pay, before they reach retirement age. This is known as 'career-long' loss, as the employee is unlikely to ever be able to pursue their career again. Although these circumstances do not come up often, career-long loss is still worth knowing about. This is because when it does come up, the calculations and disputes when dealing with it can be quite involved and complicated.

In practice, you are most likely to come across career-long loss with disability discrimination claims, older workers nearing retirement or where discrimination has led to serious psychiatric injury. In these cases, the loss will be assessed on the likelihood of the employee ever working again, either on the same or a comparable package.

The usual way for a tribunal to assess this career-long loss is using the Ogden Tables. However, even in career-long loss cases, I recommend that employers do not let the Ogden Tables have the final say. No matter how impressive (and intimidating!) the actuarial calculations may appear, there will always be uncertainty when assessing future loss, especially over a lengthy period, and the Ogden Tables do not cover every possibility.

Therefore, instead, it is well worth getting stuck into an argument with the employee about the value of the loss. No one ever knows exactly what might have happened but for the dismissal or what will happen in the future. For example, the employee may have been fairly dismissed at another time or have left voluntarily. Also, the employer may go out of business at some indeterminate point in the future – though obviously, in reality, hopefully not!

What is important when dealing with these cases is to undermine the view that the loss would have continued indefinitely. The Court of Appeal confirmed this point in *Wardle v Credit Agricole Corporate and Investment Bank [2011] IRLR 604 (CA)*. It said that a general reduction should be made, on a broad-brush basis, for the 'vicissitudes of life', for example, the possibility that the employee would have been fairly dismissed in any event or might have resigned for other reasons. The Court said it will only be appropriate to award career-long loss in rare cases where there is no real prospect of an employee ever obtaining an equivalent job. In this case, the tribunal should only have awarded compensation up to the point when there was a 'better than evens chance' the employee would find another job.

Example (no indefinite loss)

Amita was a solicitor and partner in a law firm where she worked in the global pensions team. She was unfairly dismissed as a result of sex discrimination. By the time of the tribunal hearing, she had secured a new, lower-paid (but senior) role with the government's Pensions Advisory Service.

The tribunal awarded ongoing future loss for 18 months. It held that by the end of this period there was a more than 50% chance of Amita regaining equivalent employment. The senior role at the Pensions Advisory Service would provide useful experience and contacts to help enable Amita to return to a law firm at partner level. The tribunal also took into account evidence from Amita's colleagues that she had been talking about finding a role in a national law firm in its pensions team (with less travel) before her dismissal. The possibility that she would have resigned to pursue this option was also factored into the tribunal's decision to cap the loss at 18 months.

It is worth noting that tribunals can be unsympathetic to employers who have been held responsible for a discriminatory dismissal. One of the best-known cases in this area is the Court of Appeal's decision in *Chagger v Abbey National plc [2010] IRLR 47*. The employer's evidence that the employee would have made a voluntary career move not long after his discriminatory dismissal was found to be irrelevant. The tribunal awarded the employee a total of nearly £2.8 million (plus interest), which is one of the highest awards ever made.

On appeal, the Court agreed with the tribunal's approach to calculating career-long loss and said it was realistic to assume that the employee would only have left his job for similarly remunerated new employment. It was only due to the discriminatory dismissal that the employee was left in the labour market at a time not of his choosing. He may never find an equivalent Job in those circumstances. However, the case was remitted back to the tribunal to consider whether a reduction was required to take into account the chance that Mr Chagger would have been dismissed in any event at a later date.

Similarly, in the more recent case of *Secretary of State for Justice v Plaistow UKEAT/0016/20* and *UKEAT/0085/20*, the employer's evidence was not good enough to avoid career-long loss. In that case, the employee succeeded in his claim of sexual orientation discrimination against the Prison Service. Both parties' medical experts agreed that Mr Plaistow was suffering from post-traumatic stress disorder (PTSD) and other conditions such as depression and paranoia. However, whereas Mr Plaistow's medical expert was firmly of the view that he was unlikely to work again, the employer's medical expert held a different view. The employer's medical expert could not give a definitive view on his return to work. Mr Plaistow was therefore awarded damages based on a loss of career and the likely award for this was over £2 million. This was a lot of money given that Mr Plaistow was only 41 at the time of the award.

This is a salutary lesson that where career loss damages are being claimed, you must make sure your evidence is strong. Medical evidence should deal not only with the diagnosis of the condition but also, crucially, with the prognosis. In this case, it also did not help the Prison Service that it was its own treatment of the employee that led to his injuries likely being permanent. The finding of a 'campaign' of direct discrimination and harassment involving senior prison service employees is never going to end well.

Pension loss

One thing you will need to deal with in career-loss cases is pension. This is a tricky compensation issue in its truest sense. Loss of pension can add up to very large sums in dismissal cases, particularly career-long loss. How much often depends on what type of pension the employee has, and it is crucial to establish this early on. There are many types of pensions in the UK. However, the main types likely to arise in tribunal proceedings are:

- state pension

- occupational pension

The occupational pension may be further categorised into a 'defined contribution scheme' (sometimes called a 'money purchase scheme') or a 'defined benefit scheme' (sometimes called a 'final salary scheme'). In defined contribution schemes, the employer and employee typically pay a set percentage of the employee's pay into the scheme each year. The contributions are then invested. On retirement, the employee should receive their total contributions, plus (hopefully!) a good return on their investment. However, in defined benefit schemes, the pension available to an employee on retirement is already defined in the scheme rules. The employee usually pays a set percentage of pensionable pay into the scheme each year. The employer then pays whatever further sums are required to meet the cost of the benefits accrued. With the former, the risk of market underperformance falls on the employee. With the latter, the risk of market underperformance falls on the employer.

Employees may also have their own personal pensions into which they pay contributions during their employment. However, an employer will not usually make any contributions to an employee's personal pension. This means that these schemes are unlikely to be relevant when calculating pension loss.

Having established the type of pension the employee has, the next step is to consider the loss caused by the dismissal. In respect of the state pension, a period out of work may result in a lower pension at state retirement age. This is because the state pension system depends on an individual's national insurance contributions. However, a lower state pension is relatively unusual, and the majority of an employee's loss will be in relation to occupational pension schemes.

Like any other head of loss for dismissal, the tribunal needs to assess the loss suffered that is a result of action taken by the employer. The tribunal will first consider whether it believes the employee is likely to be able to secure a job with an equally valuable pension scheme. If the employee has been a member of a defined benefit scheme, frankly these days a tribunal is unlikely to find that this will ever happen. The majority of employers have now closed their final salary schemes to new joiners. It can therefore be hard for employees lucky enough to have had a defined benefit scheme to mitigate their pension loss.

This point was illustrated in the Employment Appeal Tribunal's (EAT's) decision in *Dumfries and Galloway Council v Carroll UKEATS/0001/19/AT*. In this case, although Mr Carroll was only awarded ongoing loss of salary for six months, the EAT found his ongoing pension loss would continue until his normal retirement age of 65 and awarded approximately £145,000 in this respect (but subject to the application of the statutory cap). The tribunal was satisfied that the employee was unlikely to ever secure an equivalent final salary pension benefit in any new employment.

However, if the employee finds a new job before the tribunal hearing, it may, occasionally, break the chain of causation. This can prevent the employer being responsible for any ongoing pension loss even if the new job does not have any final salary benefits. In *Aegon UK Corporate Services Limited v Roberts [2009]*

EWCA Civ 932, the Court of Appeal held that both pension loss and future loss should be treated similarly. Therefore, where the employee finds a new job that stops the employer being responsible for future salary loss, it also stops their responsibility for any ongoing pension loss.

Given the complexities (and headaches) when dealing with pensions, it is not surprising that there has been much debate over the years as to the correct approach. In 2016, a consultation exercise was carried out by the Presidents of the Employment Tribunals to get to grips with this. The upshot was the publication in August 2017 of the *Presidential Guidance and Principles for Compensating Pension Loss*. However, since this date, the Principles have been updated several times, which helps to illustrate just how tricky this topic can be – even for the experts. The fourth edition of the Principles was published in March 2021, and it can be downloaded from https://go.danielbarnett.com/pension4.

Although tribunals are not strictly bound by the guidance, they do need to have regard to it when considering pension loss. Therefore, it's definitely worth taking a look, as it shows how the tribunal is likely to calculate this loss. The Principles also summarise the benefits of the main public sector defined benefit schemes and contain useful links to websites and extracts from the Ogden Tables. There are also plenty of good examples of how the Principles have been used in practice.

Examples of pension loss (taken from the Presidential Guidance)

• **Defined contributions:** Christopher succeeds in a complaint of unfair dismissal. He had been employed on a gross annual salary of £25,000 and his employer paid contributions of 3% into his personal pension scheme. He remains unemployed at the date of the hearing, which takes place nine months after his dismissal. The tribunal decides that he will remain unemployed for a further six months, at which point he will obtain a job at an equivalent salary and with the same level of employer pension contributions.

The award of compensation to Christopher in respect of the net pension loss arising from his unfair dismissal will be as follows:

Loss to hearing:	3% x £25,000 x 0.75 (9 months) = £562.50
Future loss:	3% x £25,000 x 0.5 (6 months) = £375.00
Total:	£937.50

• Defined contributions (lost future pay rise):
Diane succeeds in a complaint of unfair dismissal. The hearing takes place six months after her dismissal. The tribunal decides that it will take her a further nine months to obtain an alternative position with equivalent benefits. She was employed at a salary of £30,000 per annum, but the tribunal is satisfied from the evidence it hears that her salary would have increased to £35,000 three months after the hearing. Her employer contributed 5% of her salary into its defined contribution pension scheme.

The award of compensation to Diane in respect of the net pension loss arising from her unfair dismissal will be as follows:

Loss to hearing:	5% x £30,000 x 0.5 (6 months) = £750.00
Future loss:	5% x £30,000 x 0.25 (3 months) = £375.00
	5% x £35,000 x 0.5 (6 months) = £875.00
Total future loss:	£1,250.00
Total:	£2,000.00

The Principles also set out a number of assumptions for the tribunal to apply when assessing pension loss (but these aren't binding; tribunals can make different assumptions if they think it appropriate). These assumptions include:

- the employee's expected retirement age, which is assumed to be state pension age or an occupational scheme's normal retirement age

- which cases are deemed 'simple' cases – for which occupational pension scheme loss is based on employer contributions

- which cases are deemed 'complex' – for which a 'seven steps' model of assessment should be adopted, which incorporates the Ogden Tables

As the latest edition of the Principles runs to 186 pages, you may also be very pleased to know that the Judicial Pensions Working Group has produced a much shorter seven-page *Basic Guide to Compensation for Pension Loss*, which can be downloaded from https://go.danielbarnett.com/pensionsbasic. The guide aims to make the Principles more accessible to anyone trying to put a value on pension loss at an early stage of the claim.

Loss of statutory rights

Tribunals will generally award a sum for 'loss of statutory rights'. This is to compensate the employee for the fact that their continuity of employment will reset to zero with a new job, meaning they will be without the protection of some of the employment laws for a time, for example, the right to claim unfair dismissal or to qualify for a redundancy payment (which the dismissed employee won't have for the first two years in any new job). This loss is usually assessed in the region of £500.

CHAPTER 4:
Adjustments and deductions

Calculating financial loss is not all one way. Part of working out the loss involves making adjustments and deductions to ensure the employee does not get too much compensation. There are a number of adjustments and deductions that a tribunal may make in order to, for example, take account of any notice pay or ex gratia sum already received by the employee. In this chapter, I'll focus on the more significant, and trickier, examples.

Accelerated receipt

Where an employee is able to show a long-term future loss of earnings, they could receive a very large lump sum. There are obvious advantages to receiving a lot of money all in one go, particularly if the employee is younger and has many years ahead to take advantage of long-term saving rates. To counter this and make sure that the compensation is 'just and equitable', the tribunal will often adjust the lump sum to take into account this 'accelerated receipt'.

The most common way to do this is to apply the same annual discount rate that is used when calculating compensation in personal injury claims. Up to 19 March 2017, this discount rate was 2.5%. From 5 August 2019, the rate was reduced to -0.25%.

Oddly, this has the counter-intuitive effect of increasing rather than decreasing the value of claims. Therefore, given the effect of accelerated receipt actually increasing loss, courts and tribunals may be wary of applying this adjustment. It is likely, with rising inflation rates at the time of writing, that the discount rate will increase again (meaning that awards including significant sums for long-term loss get reduced to take account of the impact of receiving interest on the money).

Mitigation

The employee has a duty to take reasonable steps to reduce, or 'mitigate', their loss. This usually means looking for a new job. So, if, for example, the tribunal finds that the employee should reasonably have obtained another job within a month of their dismissal, it is likely only to award loss of earnings for one month after the dismissal. Ongoing losses after that flow from the employee's decision not to seek a new job rather than from the dismissal itself.

However, beware that the level for 'reasonable steps' to find new work is not set at a particularly high standard. By this stage, the employer has already lost at the merits hearing and the employee is now the victim of unlawful dismissal, possibly without a reference. To make it even more difficult, a tribunal will look at all the employee's circumstances, including their health and state of mind. So, if the employee suffers from ill health, this can affect their ability to mitigate.

Ultimately, it is for the employer to show that the employee has acted unreasonably, taken inadequate steps, and therefore not properly mitigated their loss. This could include, for example, providing evidence of any jobs that the employee could have applied for but did not apply for. So, it is worth investigating appropriate websites and publications to see what suitable opportunities have arisen during the employee's unemployment. Copies of these job adverts can be included in the employer's evidence at a remedy hearing. To challenge an employee's attempts to mitigate, employers must remember to compile an ongoing dossier of jobs that they believe the employee could have applied for. This is often forgotten until close to the Tribunal hearing, which puts the employer on the back foot if the gap between dismissal and the hearing is lengthy.

Where the employer is successful in proving the employee has failed to mitigate their loss, the tribunal will need to make a deduction for this. The tribunal should firstly decide when the employee would have found work if they had been searching properly. Then, it should reduce the amount of compensation by the amount of income they would have earned in that job.

Bear in mind when considering mitigation that the employee's duty only starts after the dismissal has taken effect. So, if the employee has refused an offer made before the dismissal, this does not lead to a finding they have failed to mitigate. However, if you do have the option (and can stomach it) a useful tactic to limit loss is to offer work after the dismissal. This may not always work, as the treatment of the employee or the circumstances of the dismissal may make it reasonable for them to refuse the offer. However, it is often worth a try, and it has been successful in the past, even in circumstances where the employee has been the victim of discrimination.

In the case of *Debique v Ministry of Defence UKEAT/0075/11*, the EAT upheld a tribunal's decision not to award compensation for loss of earnings to an employee who unreasonably refused an offer to transfer to a new role. Although the EAT recognised that there are discrimination cases where the employee has been so badly treated it is not fair to expect them to accept an offer of re-employment, that was not the case here. Ms Debique was a single mother serving in the British Army as a soldier and found it difficult to combine motherhood with her role. After a dispute, she gave notice and left. However, during her notice period, the Ministry of Defence offered her a new role. This role was in a unit that had childcare facilities and the Ministry also gave assurances that she would not be deployed on active service for five years.

Ms Debique turned down the role and brought claims against the Ministry of Defence for indirect race and sex discrimination. Although Ms Debique succeeded in her claims, the tribunal awarded her nothing for loss of earnings. Her refusal of the new role meant that she had failed to mitigate her loss. The tribunal found that the new role would have provided her stability and addressed her childcare difficulties too.

However, if an employer does not offer an alternative role, tribunals will generally give employees some space to get a new job at the same or similar level to their previous role. The question of how long they should continue before looking for lower-paid work is a matter for the tribunal. For example, in the case of *Yetton v Eastwoods Froy Ltd [1967] 1 WLR 104*, the employee looked for employment at the same senior level for six months before contemplating lower-paid jobs. Although the High Court suggested that the employee might have lowered their expectations earlier, it did not find that there had been any failure to mitigate. This meant the employee's losses covered the whole of that six-month period at their previous salary.

Ultimately, whether or not the employee's actions comply with the duty to mitigate will be a question of fact for the tribunal, including the economic reality at the time of the employee's job hunt and, in particular, the state of the labour market in their sector. For example, in the economic rollercoaster that followed the start of the Covid-19 pandemic, the employee's sector and the timing of their dismissal would have had a bigger impact than usual. Anyone working in the hospitality, arts and entertainment industries in the midst of a lockdown would have found it extremely difficult to find another job. However, by August 2021 employers in this industry were crying out for staff with the *CIPD Labour Market Outlook: Summer 2021* reporting that 51% of employers were reporting hard-to-fill vacancies.

For those employees who lost their jobs mid-pandemic, the lack of alternatives would no doubt have led many to retrain, change career or set up a new business venture. In most cases, this approach would have taken longer than the conventional route of job-hunting. Given this extra time, employers would most likely want to argue that this is not adequate mitigation. However, beware that all these steps may be considered reasonable by a tribunal. Indeed, to persuade a tribunal that the employee's mitigation was inadequate, an employer would likely have to show that the employee was simply turning their back on clear and certain employment opportunities. That is a pretty difficult task in normal circumstances, let alone if the employee had lost their job during the pandemic.

For example, in *Orthet Ltd v Vince-Cain [2004] IRLR 857*, the EAT held that an employee's decision to change career and undertake a four-year university course was reasonable. In this case, studying was a backup plan that the employee would only rely on if she was unable to find suitable work. The tribunal accepted her evidence that had suitable employment become available, she would have abandoned her studies to take it up. Although the employer did try to prove that there was other available work for the employee, it was unable to do so.

It may also be reasonable for an employee to mitigate their loss by starting up their own business. In the case of *Gardiner-Hill v Roland Berger Technics Ltd [1982] IRLR 498*, the EAT considered it reasonable for the employee to have spent 80% of his time setting up a new business. He had been the sole managing director of his former employer for 16 years, and it was reasonable for him to want to use that experience. If an employee does mitigate by starting a new business, then the approach to calculating their loss is a bit different.

In *Dore v Aon Ltd [2005] IRLR 891*, the Court of Appeal gave guidance that tribunals should (1) calculate what sum represents loss of earnings; (2) add any costs incurred by the employee in starting up the business; and (3) subtract any earnings from the new business.

Whatever approach an employee may take to finding new work, they will nonetheless usually be expected to apply for any state benefits to which they are entitled, such as Job Seekers' Allowance or Universal Credit. However, in unfair dismissal claims, employers need to be aware that once the tribunal proceedings are over, the *Employment Protection (Recoupment of Jobseeker's Allowance and*

Income Support) Regulations are triggered to allow the government to 'recoup' those welfare benefits. This means that the tribunal deducts the benefits from the award but orders the employer to pay back an amount equivalent to the benefits to the Department for Work and Pensions – so there is no saving to the employer.

Procedural flaws – the *Polkey* principle

Another route by which an employee's loss may be reduced is where the dismissal is only unfair due to flaws in the procedure, and the employee could have been dismissed fairly at a later date for the same or another reason.

This is referred to as the '*Polkey*' principle, taken from the House of Lords decision in *Polkey v AE Dayton Services [1987] IRLR 503*. It is only intended to put the employee in the financial position they would have been in had they been treated fairly. It would not be fair if the employee was compensated for all their loss following a dismissal in the above circumstances.

There are no formal rules for tribunals to follow when making a *Polkey* reduction. Rather, their duty is to award what is 'just and equitable'. However, in general, there are two approaches that a tribunal may take:

- **limiting the period of loss:** if the tribunal is certain that a fair dismissal was inevitable by the end of a specified period, it may award a number of weeks' pay equal to the additional length of time it would have taken to carry out a fair dismissal procedure.

- **percentage reduction:** if the tribunal is not certain that the employee would have been fairly dismissed, it should assess the percentage chance of this and reduce the losses accordingly. This percentage reduction may be anything from 0% to 100%. Where the tribunal finds that it was unlikely that the employee would have kept their job had proper procedures been followed, then the percentage reduction will be higher than if the tribunal considers that compliance with proper procedures was likely to result in the employee remaining in employment.

Examples of limiting the period of loss

Employee A is unfairly dismissed because the employer did not interview key witnesses, which meant the investigation was unreasonable. The tribunal may assess how much longer it would have taken for the employer to carry out that step and limit the award to this period. So, if it would have taken four extra weeks to interview witnesses, the compensatory award will only cover that four-week period.

Employee B is unfairly dismissed because the employer failed to follow a proper redundancy consultation procedure. The tribunal may assess how much longer it would have taken the employer to carry this out and limit the award to this period. However, in these circumstances, the tribunal should factor in the possibility of the employee being offered and accepting alternative employment during that time.

Employee C is unfairly dismissed due to sex discrimination and is unemployed long-term, resulting in substantial financial losses. However, the tribunal finds that the employee would have been fairly dismissed for misconduct six months later in any event because of their antagonistic and intransigent attitude. The employee will be awarded six months' loss of earnings, but no more (*O'Donoghue v Redcar and Cleveland Borough Council [2001] IRLR 615 (CA)*).

Examples of percentage reduction

Employee D is unfairly dismissed because the employer failed to follow a proper redundancy consultation procedure. The tribunal is not certain that the employee would have been dismissed if a fair procedure had been followed. Its assessment is that there is only a 20% chance that the employee would have avoided redundancy. In this case, the tribunal should award full compensation for the length of time it would have taken to carry out the fair procedure and then apply an 80% reduction to the compensation for losses beyond this point.

Employee E is unfairly dismissed because the employer failed to follow its performance improvement procedure. The tribunal is not certain that the employee would have been dismissed if a fair procedure had been followed. However, its assessment is that there is only a 30% chance that the employee's performance would have sufficiently improved over a six-month review period. In this case, the tribunal should reduce the compensatory award by 70%.

Tribunals are not under a general duty to investigate whether the *Polkey* principle applies to the case they are hearing. However, a tribunal must do so if there is concrete evidence to this effect, and the tribunal should consider both parties' evidence on this. The burden of proof rests with the employer to identify sufficient evidence to satisfy the tribunal that it should make a *Polkey* reduction as the employee would not have continued in employment indefinitely. The tribunal will then need to assess the chance of the employee's employment continuing. Although this is undoubtedly a tricky task, it is not one a tribunal can avoid. The tribunal is required to make some assessment, even though it may be a difficult and, to some extent, speculative exercise (*Software 2000 Ltd v Andrews and others UKEAT/0533/06*).

There is also an equivalent *Polkey* principle for discrimination claims. This is to reduce the compensation to reflect the likelihood that the employee would, in any event, have been dismissed in a non-discriminatory way. So, for example, where an employee's selection for redundancy was discriminatory, but the employer could show that the employee would have been fairly selected anyway, the employee's compensation should not include any amount that would have flowed from a non-discriminatory dismissal.

Non-compliance with the *Acas Code*

The *Acas Code* was first introduced under the *Trade Union and Labour Relations (Consolidation) Act (TULRCA) 1992*, and tribunals must take it into account when deciding on the fairness of a dismissal in certain circumstances. These situations include, for example, misconduct and poor performance, but not redundancy or the non-renewal of a limited-term contract. The *Acas Code* also applies to grievances and therefore may cover situations where the employee has resigned as a result of a grievance and claims to have been constructively dismissed, even if the situation was not 'disciplinary' in nature.

Where the employer (or the employee) has unreasonably failed to follow the *Acas Code*, the tribunal may increase (or reduce) the amount of compensation that would otherwise have been payable by no more than 25% under section 207A of TULRCA). In exercising its discretion regarding whether to make such an adjustment, the tribunal should decide whether it is 'just and equitable' to do so having regard to 'all the circumstances' of the case, including the 'size and resources of an employer'. In *Wardle v Credit Agricole Corporate and Investment Bank [2011] IRLR 604*, the Court of Appeal said that if the tribunal does decide to make an adjustment, then the extent of the uplift should be calculated in two stages:

- focus on the nature and gravity of the breach.

- consider how much that involves in monetary terms.

As the overall financial value of the uplift (or reduction) needs to be taken into account, this means that tribunals should decide on the amount of the compensatory award before turning their attention to the extent of the uplift. This is particularly important for uplifts in high-value cases where a maximum 25% uplift could add a substantial figure to the already high level of compensation awarded. This is likely to be the case in claims of discrimination where injury to feelings and aggravated damages have been awarded.

The financial value of the uplift needs to be proportionate to the gravity of the breach of the *Acas*

Code. There is no easy way to decide this, and in *Banerjee v Royal Bank of Canada UKEAT/0189/19/ JOJ*, the EAT advised that in cases where there is a risk of a disproportionate award, the tribunal should hear submissions from the parties on the extent of the uplift before fixing the appropriate percentage.

In *Slade and another v Biggs and others EA-2019- 000687* and *EA-2019-000722*, the EAT gave guidance about how to calculate the uplift and confirmed the following four-stage test:

- is it just and equitable to award any Acas uplift?

- if so, what percentage uplift is just and equitable, not exceeding but possibly equalling 25%?

- is there any overlap with other awards, such as injury to feelings, and if so, what is the appropriate adjustment, if any, to the percentage uplift to those awards in order to avoid double-counting?

- applying a final sense-check, is the sum of money represented by the application of the percentage uplift disproportionate in absolute terms? If so, what further adjustment needs to be made?

In conclusion, the EAT in *Slade* said that while wholly disproportionate sums must be scaled down, the focus remains on whether the percentage uplift is 'just and equitable in all the circumstances'.

Cases including *Acas Code* uplifts

Examples of a 25% uplift:

- the employer pursued a course of conduct to engineer the termination of two pregnant employees' employment (as their pregnancies were 'highly inconvenient'). Amongst other tactics, this included a cynical and malicious failure to comply with either the letter or the essence of the *Acas Code* when ignoring their grievances, suspending and dismissing one of the employees and insisting that the other resign (*Slade and another v Biggs and others EA-2019-000687* and *EA-2019-000722*).

- the employer failed to carry out a reasonable investigation, the outcome of the disciplinary was pre-determined and the disciplinary procedure followed while the employee was off sick was unfair (*Royal Bank of Scotland v Doherty UKEAT 0307/14*).

- the employer dismissed the employee for misconduct without giving her the opportunity to put her case at a disciplinary hearing (*Hargreaves v Wright Foundation Research Ltd* and another *ET/1804373/13*).

- a large employer with substantial administrative resources failed to carry out a reasonable investigation and the person conducting the hearing had carried out the investigation himself and was also a witness for the employer (and therefore not impartial). The specific breaches were failure to investigate properly to establish the facts; failure to interview any of the employee's witnesses; failure to give the employee written evidence and witness statements before the hearing; and failure to allow the employee to ask questions, present evidence, and call witnesses (*Bah v Pret A Manger (Europe) Ltd ET/2204635/09*).

Example of a 20% uplift:

- a large employer with substantial resources failed to give the employee proper details of the allegation and constantly interrupted him in the hearing, meaning the employee was not allowed a reasonable opportunity to respond (*Davies v Richard Preston & Son Ltd ET/2509738/09*).

Example of a 15% uplift (reduced due to the small size of the employer):

- the employer failed to follow any procedure and dismissed the employee summarily without warning for an unfair reason. The tribunal awarded a 15% uplift but said that the award was lower than it might have been

as the tribunal took into account that the
employer was a small employer who had
sought advice from Acas but had seemingly
misunderstood that advice (*Griffiths v
Treeworks (West Wales) Ltd ET/1608922/09*).

Cases including *Acas Code* reductions

Example of a 20% reduction (failure to appeal):

- the employee (unreasonably) failed to appeal
against his dismissal. The tribunal did not
apply the maximum reduction because
the employee had at least some reason for
not appealing. However, that reason (the
employee was 'disgusted' with the employer
and thought no one would overturn the
decision) was inadequate (*Baker v Birmingham
Metropolitan College ET/1301355/11*).

The other most common examples of how an
employee may (unreasonably) fail to follow the
Acas Code are:

- failure to attend a disciplinary
meeting without good cause

- failure to raise a grievance prior
to bringing a tribunal claim

Contributory fault

When dealing with unfair dismissal, the tribunal will reduce the award if it decides that the employee was in some way to blame for their dismissal. The tribunal can reduce the award by such percentage as it considers appropriate (or 'just and equitable') to reflect the employee's fault: even on occasion by 100%, but this is rare.

Contributory fault reductions are most often made in misconduct dismissals, where the tribunal believes the employee is partially to blame, but the dismissal is nonetheless unfair, for example, where a fair investigation was not carried out or the misconduct was not sufficiently serious to result in dismissal.

In *Croydon Health Services NHS Trust v Brown UKEAT/0601/11*, the employee was dismissed for gross misconduct for, amongst other things, authorising payment of invoices to a contractor without documentation. The tribunal found that the dismissal was unfair because the employer had not carried out a reasonable investigation. The EAT upheld the tribunal's finding of unfairness but said that it should have made a 25% reduction for contributory fault. In approving invoices without supporting documentation, the employee had been guilty of 'culpable or blameworthy conduct' that contributed to their dismissal.

Conduct during the course of disciplinary proceedings can also be blameworthy and may justify a finding of contributory fault, for example, being dishonest or falsely accusing others of dishonesty.

However, 'general' blameworthy conduct by the employee will not necessarily lead to a reduction. The conduct does need to contribute to the dismissal. In *Nejjary v Aramark Ltd UKEAT/0054/12*, a hospitality manager was dismissed following a client complaint about the organisation of a breakfast meeting. The tribunal made a 100% deduction for contributory fault which not only took the employee's behaviour in respect of the breakfast meeting into account but also other aspects of his employment record unrelated to the dismissal. The EAT held that this was not right. The tribunal should only have taken into account the blameworthy conduct that contributed to the dismissal.

As it is the blameworthy behaviour of the employee that is in question, it is rare for a tribunal to reduce an award for contributory fault in capability or sickness absence dismissals (because generally, the employee is not 'blameworthy' – they're just unfortunate or not up to standard). Also, contributory fault reductions will only be made in respect of the employee's acts that occurred before the dismissal. Post-dismissal conduct is irrelevant.

However, reductions for pre-dismissal blameworthy behaviour can be made, even where the employer was not aware of this at the time. For example, in *Phoenix House v Stockman [2016] IRLR 848*, the EAT confirmed the tribunal's decision to reduce the compensatory award by an additional 10%. This was because the employee had made a covert recording before her dismissal of a meeting with the employer's Director of Human Resources. The employer only found out about this after the dismissal and during the tribunal proceedings.

CHAPTER 5:
Types of discrimination awards

Unlike unfair dismissal compensation, which is limited to financial loss, discrimination compensation can also cover non-financial losses. In most cases, this will take the form of an injury to feelings award, but it may also include an award for personal injury and aggravated damages.

Injury to feelings

The *Equality Act 2010* (sections 119 and 124) provides that a tribunal can make an award, unrelated to financial loss, for injured feelings resulting from discriminatory treatment. The award is to compensate the victim for the hurt caused by their mistreatment, rather than to punish the employer. Therefore, the amount of compensation should not be so high as to amount to a windfall. On the other hand, tribunals should avoid awards that are too low, as they risk not properly recognising injured feelings.

Due to the vague nature of these awards, in 2003, the Court of Appeal provided guidelines in *Vento v. Chief Constable of West Yorkshire (No 2) [2003] IRLR 102*. It set out three rough 'bands' of awards.

At the time of writing, the bands are as follows (for claims brought between 6 April 2022 and 5 April 2023; they increase every year on 6 April to account for inflation):

- a lower band of £990 to £9,900 (for less serious cases, usually involved a one-off act of discrimination)

- a middle band of £9,900 to £29,600 (for serious cases not worthy of an upper band award, usually because the discrimination is of moderate term in duration. Most dismissals fall into this category.)

- an upper band of £29,600 to £49,300 (for the most serious cases), with the most exceptional cases capable of exceeding £49,300.

These bands are extremely helpful, and tribunals now routinely refer to them when making their awards. However, even then, it can be very difficult to predict the award a tribunal may make and, in practice, injury to feelings awards vary greatly.

When assessing an injury to feelings award, the tribunal will focus on the effect the conduct has on the employee. It will look at the degree of hurt, distress or upset caused rather than the gravity of the discrimination. Also, the tribunal will take the victim as it finds them. It is about how the particular employee reacts to the discrimination and not about how they should have reacted. So, even if the employer thinks the employee's reaction is disproportionate and they shouldn't be so upset, this won't help.

Other relevant factors when assessing the award include:

- any medical condition from which the employee is suffering

- the position of the person who was found to be discriminating

- the nature of the employee's job and the effect the discrimination has on their career

- the way in which the employer dealt with any grievance brought by the employee

Whether the discrimination was a one-off incident or a course of conduct will also be relevant. One-off incidents are likely to fall into the lower *Vento* band and a course of conduct in the middle or upper bands. However, it is not decisive. A particularly serious and offensive one-off incident could be in the middle band (indeed, dismissal – which is a one-off act – often falls into this category). Equally, minor but continuing discrimination could fall within the lower band. It is the effect on the employee that is important.

When it comes to the injury to feelings award, the burden is on the employee to establish the fact and extent of their distress. However, the employee does not necessarily need to present medical evidence as it is not a question of a diagnosed injury. It is more about understanding the hurt caused to the employee by the discrimination and deciding an appropriate amount to compensate for this.

The good news is that the tribunal's assessment of injury to feelings awards should not be influenced by its disapproval of the employer's unlawful conduct. In *Corus Hotels plc v Woodward and another UKEAT/0536/05*, the EAT held that a tribunal had allowed its 'feelings of indignation' at the employer's conduct to inflate the injury to feelings award. Happily, for the employer, the EAT reduced the award from £5,000 to £4,000.

However, the bad news is that serious incidents of an employer's discrimination will likely mean an award in the upper *Vento* band. To give you a worst-case scenario example, in the case of *Anne Giwa Amu v Department for Work and Pensions 1600465/2017*, the tribunal made a total compensatory award of over £200,000. She was awarded an overall injury to feelings award in the upper *Vento* band of £35,000 (of which £7,500 was aggravated damages) plus interest. The high level of award reflected the tribunal's upholding of 12 complaints of direct discrimination, victimisation or harassment relevant to race and/or age. It found that the Department for Work and Pensions staff had deliberately created a 'hostile environment' that had left the employee feeling entirely rejected, ridiculed and isolated.

Examples of injury to feelings awards

- **Upper band:**

  o award of £30,000: the employee suffered a series of discriminatory acts over a period of about two years due to pregnancy. The Managing Director made numerous disparaging remarks about her pregnancy, including that she would be 'hopeless' and 'never the same again'. He reduced his support and contact with her, gave her an unfairly critical appraisal and asked her to resign. She was not appointed to the Board of Directors and her associate membership of the Institute of Directors was cancelled. She was demoted, her benefits were removed and during her second pregnancy, there was a continuing campaign to persuade her not to return to work. Unsurprisingly, the tribunal upheld her discrimination claim and said that 'it is not often these days that the tribunal is faced with such a blatant response to notification of pregnancy'. The length of time over which the acts took place and the impact on her as a pregnant woman meant an *upper band award was appropriate (Manning v Safetell and Medlam (ET/1100434/07 and ET/1101662/07)).*

- **Middle band:**

  - award of £16,000 (for a one-off act): the employee was employed for three months until she was unexpectedly dismissed for a (false) reason of redundancy. When she sought to challenge this reason, she was intimidated by her managers in a way that she clearly found upsetting. She was also later depressed for three months. She brought a race discrimination claim. Shortly before the tribunal hearing, the employer changed the reason for dismissal to misconduct due to theft. The tribunal did not accept this reason and held that the employee had been discriminated against. On appeal, the EAT confirmed that in this case, the single act of discrimination (the dismissal) was serious enough to justify an award in the middle band (*Base Childrenswear Ltd v Otshudi UKEAT/0267/18*).

  - award of £10,000: the employee, a chef, was diagnosed with pancreatic cancer. When he told his employer about his cancer diagnosis, he was summarily dismissed. He brought a claim for disability discrimination and the tribunal upheld this. The tribunal found his dismissal was unfavourable treatment and that this had been very upsetting for him. The dismissal also meant the loss of his home, which was provided to him by the employer as part of his employment. There were also other stresses in his life, including issues with his wife's pension and longstanding health problems. The employee was diagnosed with depression and prescribed anti-depressant medication for the first time in his life (*Mr Z Baran v Mario Iasi and Salvatore Iasi t/a Bel-Vedere Ristorante Italiano (Case No 3306950/2018)*).

- **Lower band:**

  o award of £2,500: the employee was a sales manager in a perfume marketing business. The owner of the business commented (in the employee's absence) that she did not understand the UK market because she was not English. He said she did not have credibility with buyers because she was Romanian, which was why she could not close deals with customers. The employee succeeded in her tribunal claim for race discrimination. The comments and the way he said them were found to be offensive, and when they were relayed to the employee, she was considerably upset. However, the injury to feelings award was in the lower band because the comments were not made directly to her or made deliberately to upset her. Further, she did not make any immediate complaint about them (*Duinea v Intertrade Holding Ltd (Reading) (Case No 2221708/2009)*).

Additionally, when the employee reported her concerns about being bullied, managers breached her confidence by talking to staff about it. This is undoubtedly a scenario to avoid. A further note of caution is that the EAT is generally reluctant to interfere with a tribunal's award. This is because it is the tribunal and not the EAT that has heard the evidence.

Personal injury

In most cases, the degree of stress and depression caused by discrimination is compensated as 'injury to feelings'. However, where the employer's actions have caused a recognised and diagnosed psychiatric injury, there should be a separate personal injury award for this. That said, if separate awards are made, tribunals must be careful to avoid double recovery. The aim of the compensatory award is to compensate for the loss suffered, not to provide a windfall.

The distinction was recognised as a tricky line to tread by the EAT in *HM Prison Service v Salmon [2001] IRLR 425*. The facts of this case involved severe sexual harassment and extreme derogatory treatment of a female prison officer by some of her male colleagues. She was deeply upset and shocked, and she was diagnosed as suffering from a moderate to severe depressive illness. She eventually took medical retirement. The tribunal awarded £11,250 compensation for personal injury in respect of psychiatric damage caused to her, in addition to

£20,000 for injury to feelings. On appeal, the EAT acknowledged that in principle, injury to feelings and psychiatric injury are separate but that in practice, it can be difficult to identify when the distress and humiliation suffered becomes a recognised psychiatric illness.

In this case, the employee's psychiatric injury was distinguishable from her injury to feelings and separate awards were appropriate without double recovery. However, where it is too difficult to separate the injuries, the EAT saw nothing wrong with tribunals treating the personal injury as having been compensated for by an injury to feelings award, so long as the tribunal identifies those aspects of the employee's medical condition that the award is intended to cover.

Employees need to be aware that if the tribunal makes a judgment on personal injury, they will most likely lose the right to bring the claim in the civil courts.

There are two types of damages available for personal injury claims:

- **general damages:** this is intended to cover such things as pain, suffering and loss of mental or physical capacity. These damages are calculated in accordance with the *Judicial Studies Board Guidelines for the Assessment of General Damages in Personal Injury Cases*. These guidelines are used by all judges in personal injury cases and give guidance on appropriate levels of award for different degrees of illness and the factors to consider.

- **special damages:** these are available for financial loss, such as medical expenses and loss of earnings. However, these will normally be dealt with when assessing financial loss as a result of the discrimination itself. Also, if an employee is unlikely to work again due to the injury, the tribunal may use the Ogden Tables to calculate the loss – along with the complicated multipliers.

An employer will be liable to pay compensation for the psychiatric injury to the extent that their unlawful discrimination has caused it. In *Essa v Laing Ltd [2004] EWCA Civ 2*, the Court of Appeal decided that an employee who suffered deliberate racial abuse at work could receive compensation for any loss arising 'naturally and directly from that wrong'. There is no need for the psychiatric injury to be reasonably foreseeable.

However, there are limits to this. It should at least be reasonably foreseeable that an injury could arise from the discrimination, even if the particular type of harm is not foreseeable. Additionally, the case in question concerned deliberate direct discrimination. It may be that in cases of indirect discrimination or inadvertent harassment, the employee would still need to show the injury was reasonably foreseeable.

If the employer's discrimination was only one of the factors that caused the personal injury, the compensation should be reduced to reflect only the ill health caused by the discrimination. This is known as 'apportionment', and it can get tricky when trying to unpick what caused which aspect of the employee's condition. The extra expense of a medical report from an expert is well worth it here. However, do make sure that the report is clear.

In *Olayemi v Athena Medical Centre and Okoreaffia UKEAT/0140/15*, the employee, who suffered PTSD, succeeded in her claim for sex discrimination and was awarded over £750,000 for sex discrimination, unfair dismissal and breach of contract. However, the employer successfully persuaded the tribunal to make a 12.5% reduction to the award as a previous episode of PTSD (related to abusive behaviour by her neighbours) had contributed to her current condition.

The EAT overturned this reduction. It found that the joint expert report had been inconsistent in dealing with the role played by the previous PTSD. It was unclear whether the employee was predisposed to PTSD or whether the previous episode had, in fact, caused her current illness.

Paying for a (hopefully good) expert report is probably the least expensive option for employers when dealing with personal injury claims. It can get very expensive, particularly as the employer needs 'to take the victim as they find them'. Similar to injury to feelings, the compensation is calculated more on the effect on the individual and less on the nature of the discrimination itself. If the discrimination has a seriously adverse effect, for example, it causes a nervous breakdown, it will not really matter that it might have affected another employee less.

Just to give an extreme example, both in respect of the amount of money a personal injury claim could cost and the amount of psychiatric harm an employee could suffer, consider the case of *Michalak v Mid-Yorkshire Hospitals NHS Trust and others ET/1810815/08*. This was a race and sex discrimination case involving a hospital consultant. Given the decent salary level and highly prized public sector final salary pension, it was already going to be expensive for the Trust.

The Trust lost the case. The tribunal found that several of its employees had campaigned against the employee over a lengthy period of time. The tribunal also accepted the joint medical experts' evidence that, as a result of her discriminatory treatment, the employee had been left with PTSD, chronic anxiety, depression and a personality change. The medical evidence also stated that she would never work in any professional capacity again, so it was a 'career-loss' case. The tribunal awarded £56,000 for psychiatric injury in view of its 'enduring' effect on her personality, on top of the then maximum £30,000 for injury to feelings. So, if ever you needed another reason to avoid discriminatory treatment in the workplace, there it is!

Aggravated damages

Sometimes, the pain for an employer can be added to further by an award of aggravated damages. Thankfully, this is a smaller sum, not often above £5,000. These damages are awarded if an employer's conduct has been exceptionally high-handed, malicious, insulting or oppressive. While it is not supposed to be a punishment for the employer's conduct, in reality, it is. However, there does need to be a link between the aggravating act complained of and the injury or loss suffered by the employee. Examples of employers' actions that could lead to aggravated damages include:

- the manner of conducting internal procedures, including failure to investigate complaints or take them seriously

- promoting or otherwise rewarding the employees who have discriminated against the employee

- continuing failure to correct a problem that has led to the discrimination

- failure to apologise to an employee who remains in employment

An example where a substantial amount was awarded for aggravated damages is the case of *Zaiwalla & Co and another v Walia UKEAT/451/00* and *UKEAT/827/00*. The case involved the unreasonable conduct of a firm of solicitors (who you would have thought would know better). The firm was found to have discriminated against the employee, a trainee solicitor, on grounds of sex. It also conducted its defence of the tribunal proceedings in a manner deliberately designed to be intimidating and threatening and to cause maximum distress. The tribunal awarded the employee £43,149, including aggravated damages of £7,500, as well as an injury to feelings award of £15,000. The employer appealed the level of award. However, the EAT confirmed that the tribunal had been entitled to make the award, particularly in respect of aggravated damages.

You may be pleased to know that the EAT did say that this case involved 'exceptional' litigation misconduct that went beyond the usual level of 'lively' dispute between the parties.

Exemplary damages

Exemplary damages are intended to punish the employer rather than compensate the employee, and they are also fittingly known as 'punitive' damages. However, they are only available in very limited cases where the compensation itself is insufficient punishment. The aim is to use the damages as a marker of the tribunal's disapproval of the employer's conduct and to deter any repetition. The employer's conduct must be either:

- oppressive, arbitrary or unconstitutional action by the agents of the government, or

- calculated to make a profit that may well exceed the compensation otherwise payable to the employee.

In practice, in an employment context, awards have generally only been made in the first category. Therefore, unless the employer is in the public sector and there is evidence that it acted oppressively, arbitrarily or unconstitutionally, such damages are unlikely to come up. Even if the employer is in the public sector and there is such evidence, there is still a high threshold to meet. The EAT held in the case of *Ministry of Defence v Fletcher UKEAT/0044/09* that 'exemplary damages are to be reserved for the most serious abuses of government power'.

A case in which such a threshold was met was *Michalak* (referred to in the 'Personal injury' section above), in which the tribunal held that the employer NHS Trust (as a public body) was exercising a power 'analogous to ... governmental functions' when it used its disciplinary powers over a hospital consultant under the Department of Health's Maintaining High Professional Standards (MHPS) policy framework. In failing to follow the MHPS, the Trust had acted in a manner that was not merely discriminatory but also 'oppressive, arbitrary or unconstitutional'. The tribunal held that it was appropriate to punish this conduct with exemplary damages of £4,000, which it added to the compensation for injury to feelings, psychiatric injury and financial loss.

A tribunal reached a similar decision involving a consultant surgeon in *Palmer v East and North Hertfordshire NHS Trust ET/1202802/09*. The tribunal awarded £5,000 exemplary damages for the Trust's 'truly shocking sustained, arbitrary and outrageous use of the executive [i.e., the NHS]'. This award was made in addition to compensation for injury to feelings of £15,000 and aggravated damages of £5,000, as the Trust's actions were found to be motivated 'by malice or spite' and it had repeatedly refused to issue an apology.

CHAPTER 6:
Tax and the statutory cap

This is probably one of the trickiest issues, and it has caused many headaches. Although the employee's losses are calculated on a net basis, they are liable to pay tax and national insurance on any tribunal award over £30,000 (except for injury to feelings). Therefore, any award for more than this amount needs to be 'grossed up' and the resulting tax payment made to HMRC.

Example 1: Calculating tax

Employee A has net losses of £36,000 and falls into the higher rate tax bracket (40%).

The first £30,000 can be paid tax free. However, for the balance of £6,000, tax has to be taken into account as the employee needs to receive the £6,000 net after the payment of tax by the employer. This means the tribunal has to work out what amount (the gross sum), after deducting tax at 40%, leaves the remaining 60% as £6,000.

This gross sum is calculated by multiplying the net sum of £6,000 by 10/6 (or 10÷6). (For the maths-minded among you, the reason is that the gross sum multiplied by 6/10 (or 60%) gives you the net sum of £6,000, so to work out the gross sum from the net sum, you need to multiply the net sum by 10/6.)

In this example, £6,000 (net) x 10/6 = £10,000 (gross sum). This means the total award to be paid by the employer is £40,000 (£30,000 (tax free) + £10,000). When 40% tax is paid on the £10,000, there is £6,000 left, meaning the employee receives the correct award of £36,000 (the £30,000 tax free + the £6,000).

Employee B is in the higher rate tax bracket (40%) and has net losses of £90,000.

The balance of their net loss over £30,000 is £60,000, and tax has to be taken into account for this amount. The tribunal will work out the gross sum (using the formula explained in respect of Employee A). So, £60,000 (net) x 10/6 = £100,000 (gross). This means the total award is £130,000 (£30,000 (tax free) + £100,000), but this is subject to the statutory cap (see below).

Once any loss over £30,000 is grossed up, the final stage (for straightforward unfair dismissal claims at least) is to add that amount to the tax-free element and apply the statutory cap.

As the cap is currently set at £93,878 (or one year's gross pay where lower), it does not make any difference for lower earners as the total compensatory award is likely to be less than this amount. However, for high earners, or those who otherwise have a high level of loss, the application of the cap to the grossed-up sum can be pretty punishing. The case law is clear that it is not possible to gross up above the cap. This means that it is never possible for a high earner to actually recover their true loss.

Example 2: applying the statutory cap

Following on from Example 1, the next step is to apply the statutory cap. This is currently £93,878. The tax owed to HMRC will need to be paid out of this award.

For **Employee A** the statutory cap makes no difference as the award of £40,000 is below the cap amount. The employer pays £4,000 of this award in tax to HMRC and the balance of £36,000 to the employee.

For **Employee B** the statutory cap makes a difference here as the employee's award of £130,000 is reduced by the cap to £89,493. From this, the employee receives £30,000 tax free, which reduces the amount to £59,493. This remaining amount is subject to tax at 40% (approximately

---

£23,500), which is paid to HMRC, and the employer pays the employee the balance of approximately £36,000. This means the employee receives £66,000 (£30,000 + £36,000).

Without the application of the statutory cap, the employee would have received £90,000.

It gets even worse if the employee has been unlucky enough to have already used their £30,000 tax-free amount in that tax year – for example, they may already have received a redundancy payment – as the whole sum will be taxed and capped in these circumstances.

APPENDIX
UNFAIR DISMISSAL
SCHEDULE OF LOSS

Case No: 24410525/2022

B E T W E E N:

JANET SMITH

Claimant

-and-

CHEQUERS MANAGEMENT COMPANY LIMITED

Respondent

SCHEDULE OF LOSS

Date of Birth:	25 February 1977
Start Date:	29 November 2017
Termination Date:	4 February 2022
Age at Termination Date:	44
Tribunal Hearing Date:	12 December 2022

Salary (gross)	£45,000pa or £865pw
Salary (net at 2021/22 rates)	£34,262pa or £659pw

The Claimant obtained a new job on 1 May 2022 on a salary of £39,500pa gross (net equivalent £30,189pa or £581pw).

Basic Award

4 complete years' employment, of which:

3 years x £544 max week's pay (2021/22 rates) x 1.5 (3 years' service over 41)	£2,448
1 year x £544 max week's pay (2021/22 rates) x 1.0 (1 year's service between 22 and 41)	£544
Total	£2,992

Compensatory Award

5 February 2022 to 30 April 2022 12 weeks @ £659pw	£7,908
1 May 2022 to 12 December 2022 (hearing date) 32 weeks @ £78pw (£659 less £581 new earnings)	£2,496
Future Loss after tribunal hearing Say 12 months' future loss (£34,262 less £30,189)	£4,073
Loss of statutory rights	£500
Total	£14,977
Total Basic plus Compensatory Award	**£17,969**

Also by
Daniel Barnett

Available on Amazon
or visit
go.danielbarnett.com/books

JOIN DANIEL EVERY SATURDAY EVENING AT
9PM WHEN HE PRESENTS THE ALL-NEW

LBC LEGAL HOUR

— OR CATCH UP VIA THE GLOBAL PLAYER,
AT bit.ly/lbclegalhour

SATURDAYS, 9PM

IMMEDIATE ACCESS
TO PRAGMATIC & PRACTICAL
HR & EMPLOYMENT LAW ADVICE
YOU CAN
IMMEDIATELY
PUT TO USE FROM
THE SHARPEST THOUGHT LEADERS
& HR PROFESSIONALS IN THE UK

FROM THE DESK OF DANIEL BARNETT

May 2022

Dear HR Professional,

You've got so many things going on at work.

The tricky HR issues you have to handle take up your time, your energy and your brain power. It can be exhausting to work under that level of pressure.

Maintaining your high standards of professionalism can be a real struggle, especially when your efforts and expertise often go unappreciated.

You have to make decisions on challenging HR situations you've sometimes never encountered before. Even if you're part of a team, it can feel like you're working in isolation.

With so much complexity and ambiguity, it's not always clear whether you're doing the right thing when there is so much to think about.

It can be draining. You've got to make tough decisions which may be unpopular. You need to ensure people are treated fairly while the business complies with its legal obligations. You've got pressure coming at you from all sides.

Doubt can creep in. What if you've got it wrong? You might even begin to question yourself.

You've got to cope with all that, whilst constantly having to convince any doubting stakeholders you're adding value to the business.

That's where the HR Inner Circle comes in. It's designed to ease that pressure by giving you swift access to resources and practical guidance you can implement right away.

Information I know that saves you time, energy and effort; resources packed full of practical, actionable advice that's difficult to find anywhere else; and a vibrant, active community of caring, like minded HR professionals willing to help you.

It's so easy to find what you want. And it doesn't matter what you're working on.

Whether it be workforce engagement, attracting and keeping talent, diversity and inclusion or employee health and well being, you'll find support for all of that.

You're covered even if you're working on one of those tricky, sensitive, people problems you never see coming until they land squarely on your plate.

Timely Support To Make Your Job Easier, Can Be Rapidly Found In The HR Inner Circle

As a member of the HR Inner Circle, all you have to do is ask. Or just do a quick search in the members' area (more about how easy that is in a moment).

Your first port of call is the vibrant Facebook group, bursting at the seams with incredible HR professionals like you. Just post your question and let it bubble and simmer in the collective genius of the group.

By the end of the day, you'll have at least 3-5 comments on your post, often more. You'll get relevant, insightful and practical guidance that comes from the hard earned experience of your fellow members.

Often you'll get a response within a couple of hours. Sometimes you'll get an answer within minutes - even if it's late in the evening!

This highly active community never fails to astound with just how willing they are to help fellow HR professionals like you by sharing their knowledge and experience.

> *"Just Join. The Information and updates from the HR Inner Circle are excellent as well as the Facebook group where you can ask other members for advice which if you work alone is great as sometimes you just need to sense-check things."*
>
> **Nicky Gleadow, HR Professional**

> *"If you're looking for a forum to discuss confidential issues and need prompt employment law advice then the HR Inner Circle is definitely for you. In addition it offers other tools to help and support. The Facebook group is full of information and solutions to scenarios invaluable for HR professionals".*
>
> **Sheena Doyle, HR Professional**

While you wait for your answer from the Facebook group, you can also search the members' vault in our secure online portal. It takes just 2 clicks and a quick keyword search using our Rapid Results Search Tool.

Instantly, you'll find exactly where your topic is covered in our extensive back catalogue of monthly magazines and audio seminars. One more click and you're straight there. In under 30 seconds you can find exactly what you're after. It's that quick and easy.

If you need a specific legal insight, pose your question live to an expert employment lawyer in our monthly Q&A session.

It'll either be me or one of my prominent contemporaries. Get your answer immediately without having to pay any legal costs.

A quick search of the previous Q&A sessions, and you'll find where it's been answered before. Our clever index system means you can find a question, and in one click get straight to the answer.

But perhaps you need to dive deep and explore the different options open to you?

Then join one of our monthly HR Huddles. There you can run your specific situation past other HR professionals. They'll offer their insights, share their experience and work WITH you to find a solution that works FOR you.

It's A Labour Of Love Putting All This Together For You.

I've spent years practising law and have become recognised as one of the UK's leading employment law barristers. I've even got my own radio show! But more importantly for you, I've also developed another skill.

It's bringing employment expertise AND practical experience together in a way that supports busy, overworked (and sometimes stressed) HR professionals like you.

Being a member now means your business and clients will see you as even more informed about the intricacies of employment law. They'll marvel at how well you keep up to date when you're so busy working hard for them.

You'll be seen making quicker decisions and implementing solutions that will accelerate the growth of the organisation. You'll make impressive time and cost savings for the business.

And those tricky, off-piste situations you've never come across before? Well, nothing will faze you, because you're backed up by an HR support system second to none.

But more importantly, you'll feel that pressure gently ease off.

That's Why I'm Inviting You To Reap The Many Rewards Of Membership

Here's what you get when you join the HR Inner Circle:

 Firstly, you'll get unlimited access to the hugely popular HR Inner Circle Facebook Private Group (Value: £1,188.00 a year)

- Tap into the vast wealth of knowledge, experience, insight and wisdom of the top 0.5% of your profession at any time, day or night.

- In less than 5 minutes you can post ANY HR question and get insightful answers and suggestions in a couple of hours or less, from some of the best in your profession.

- Fast track your impact by discovering effective shortcuts and workarounds from people who've been "there" and done "it".

- Expand and deepen your network of like minded individuals, secure in the knowledge they're as dedicated and as ambitious as you.

- Increase your prestige with your colleagues and stakeholders by being part of such an exclusive and prominent HR community.

- Gain confidence in your judgment and decisions by using the highly responsive community as a sounding board for your ideas.

"The HR Inner Circle is fantastic support for HR Professionals. The Facebook group is a great sense check when you work on your own and a great way to get a different perspective.."

Nancy Prest, HR Professional

"The HR Inner Circle is the best CPD investment you can make. Regardless of how you learn best, there is something for everyone and you're always up to date about employment law, case law and the subtle gray areas in between. If it's not already written down, just ask the group and someone will have the answer."

Lara Kenny, HR Professional

"The HR Inner Circle is an extremely helpful forum in which to bounce around ideas with very knowledgeable and experienced HR professionals and ask for advice and views on employment relations issues."

Yolaine Bech, HR Professional

2 **Secondly, you'll receive 11 copies of the HR Inner Circular Magazine every year (Value: £350.00 annual subscription)**

- Enjoy that satisfying "THUD" on your door mat every month when the postman delivers your very own copy of the HR Inner Circular magazine.

- Quickly discover exactly what the law says about key issues affecting HR professionals around the UK who are just like you.

- Get concise and practical guidance on how employment law applies to the challenging situations and circumstances you deal with every day.

- Avoid the mistakes of others by applying the lessons from the in depth analysis of real life case studies.

- Benefit from a legal deep dive by the UK's leading employment law barrister into a topical employment question posed by a fellow member (perhaps you!).

- Review a summary of recent important Facebook Group discussions worthy of sharing, that you may have missed.

- Learn from a range of related and relevant topics useful for your practice and your broader professional development.

"I thoroughly recommend the HR Inner Circle. It's worth every penny from the monthly magazine to the weekly podcast to the monthly audio seminars. And just having the support network to call on for a comfort blanket from time to time. I've been a member since it started"

Alison Melville, HR Professional

> *"The HR Inner Circle Magazine is really informative, the Facebook group is such a community and I think exceptional value for money."*
>
> **Lis Moore, HR Professional**

3 **Thirdly, you get an exclusive invite to a live online Q&A Session every month, led by an expert employment lawyer (Value: £199.00 a session or £2,388 a year)**

- Gain 60 minutes of live and direct access to the sharpest legal minds from my secret little black book of contacts.

- Get answers to your knottiest employment law questions, and solutions to your trickiest HR problems, from some of the brightest employment lawyers in the UK.

- Avoid having to pay the £300-£400 it would cost you to ask a lawyer your question outside of the HR Inner Circle.

- Benefit from valuable insights from the answers given to other members.

- If you can't attend live, watch the recording when it's convenient for you.

- Quickly access the recorded answer to any question asked in the session by simply clicking the question index for that session.

- Save time by downloading the session transcription to scan-read at a time suitable for you.

"The HR Inner Circle gives you access to Daniel's practical and straightforward advice on employment issues. The businesses I work with don't want jargon, they just want pragmatic advice and I can access that through HR Inner Circle"

Mandy Carr, HR Professional

"It's a breath of fresh air to have an HR resource which gives practical advice and tips. We can find out the law but it's the application of the law and HR practice led by a barrister along with the opinions of other HR professionals in the Q&A sessions which are invaluable "

Caroline Robertson, HR Professional

 Fourthly, Join a live Monthly Huddle with other HR Professionals to solve your most challenging HR problems (Value: £1,188.00 a year)

- Attend your very own mini-mastermind group of highly qualified, highly regarded and experienced fellow HR professionals to "group think" through an issue you're facing right now.

- Develop bespoke solutions to the unique problems and challenges you have to deal with in a safe, supportive and confidential environment.

- Feel safe knowing these online zoom calls are NOT recorded to respect the sensitivity of issues addressed and the privacy of those involved. [NOTE - a professional transcriber attends and takes written notes. An anonymised summary is then made available to the membership]

- Recent Huddle topics included changing employee benefits, mandatory vaccination, career breaks, sickness during disciplinaries, effective worker forums and hybrid working arrangements.

"The HR Inner Circle is a great network opportunity to get practical and refreshing approaches for day to day HR and employment law matters. It's great to see that we all experience tricky cases from time to time"

Annabel Carey, HR Professional

"HR can be a lonely role and as the person advising everyone around you, it can often be difficult to find advice and peer support for you as an individual. We all know there are rarely right and wrong answers in HR. It's an art not a science and the HR Inner Circle gives you a group of like minded individuals to share solutions, provide expertise and insight, and a place to go when you just don't have the answers. "

Jo Mosley, HR Professional

> *"Lots of HR professionals work in standalone in-house roles or their own consultancy. We all need to stay relevant and get an occasional sanity check on a project and bounce around ideas and problems off others. So joining the HR Inner Circle to find a group of like minded professionals is essential in my view."*

Vanessa Scrimshaw, HR Professional

5 And finally, Your Personal Concierge will help you get the best out of your membership (Value: Priceless!)

- You get personal access to a personal concierge who'll point you in the direction of exactly where to find what you need. She's supported hundreds of members over the years she's been at my side.

- She also works closely with the 11 back office staff that support the operation. In the extremely unlikely event she doesn't know where something is, she knows who will.

> *"Use everything in the HR Inner Circle and you'll get the best possible support. The Magazine and the Audio Seminars keep me up to date and I can give something back and learn a few things on the Facebook group."*

Michelle Kirk, HR Professional

"The Inner Circle is a forum where you can get HR advice in all different formats. The monthly magazines and the audio seminars, the Facebook group and the annual conference. It is excellent value for money."

Christine Cooper, HR Professional

"Just join. The resources available to the HR Inner Circle members are invaluable especially the Facebook group where you can get advice or a different point of view that you may not have previously considered outside of normal working hours which is really useful. Live Q&As too."

Diana Wilks, HR Professional

How Much Does joining the HR Inner Circle Cost?

Let me remind you of the annual value of membership you get when you join:

Access to the private Facebook Group	£ 1,188.00
HR Inner Circular Magazine subscription	£ 350.00
Live Q&A sessions	£ 2,388.00
Monthly HR Huddles	£ 1,188.00
Your Personal Membership Concierge	PRICELESS!

TOTAL £ 5,114.00

But you're not going to pay anywhere near that. **All it's going to cost you is just £96 +VAT per month. That's the equivalent of the price of a daily Starbucks.**

Another way of looking at your investment is this:

It's like having your very own part time, legally trained, assistant HR Business Partner, just waiting to provide you with all the answers you need…. **all for just £96+VAT per month.**

And that price is fixed for as long as you remain a member.

Plus, With Membership Of The HR Inner Circle, You'll Also Get These 6 Bonuses
Worth £3,305.00 For FREE!

Bonus #1: Free Access To The Annual Conference every May (Value: £399)
The perfect opportunity to extend your personal network and gather key insights and takeaways to help you personally and professionally. Includes lunch too.

Bonus #2 - Monthly Audio Seminars (Value: £588.00)
A 60 minute legal deep dive by me into an important subject relevant to you and your practice every month (downloadable mp3).

Bonus #3 - Handling Awkward Conversations (Value: £997.00)
A video case study masterclass you can share with managers to train them to handle awkward staff disciplinary, performance and attitude problems.

Bonus #4 - 4 x HR Employment Online Courses (Value: £388.00)

Deconstructing TUPE, Changing Terms & Conditions, Unconscious Bias At Work and Handling Grievances.

Bonus #5 - Free listing on the Register of Investigators (Value: £250.00)

Advertise your professional investigations service in our member's portal

Bonus #6 - Significant Discounts On My Flagship Products (Value: £683.00)

Get member discounts on my Getting Redundancy Right and HR Policies products as well as other price reductions as new products are released.

I'm So Confident Joining The HR Inner Circle Is The Right Decision For You, Here's My 100% Satisfaction "Buy It Back" Guarantee

Take action and join the HR Inner Circle now. If you're not 100% satisfied with your investment after 30 days, I'll refund and buy EVERYTHING back from you.

I'm comfortable doing this because I know once you join, you'll find the support, the information and the strategies so useful, you'll never want to leave.

Before you decide though, let me be very clear about membership of the HR Inner Circle.

It's only for ambitious and dedicated HR professionals who want to accelerate and increase their impact by plugging into an HR ecosystem with its finger firmly on the pulse of what's working right now in HR. If you're just plodding along and are content with just getting by, then this is probably not for you.

But if you're drawn to benefiting from standing shoulder to shoulder with some of the giants in the HR community, then re-joining the HR Inner Circle is the RIGHT decision for you. Join here now:

www.hrinnercircle.co.uk

Daniel Barnett

PS after you join www.hrinnercircle.co.uk, if you don't feel it's right for you, we'll refund anything you've paid if you ask within 30 days.

If you are looking for a forum to discuss confidential issues that need prompt employment law advice, then the HR Inner Circle is definitely for you. In addition it offers other tools to help and support. The Facebook group is full of information and solutions to scenarios — invaluable for HR professionals.

- **Sheena Doyle**, Managing Director, The Really Useful HR Company Ltd

It's a forum where you're not afraid to ask stupid questions, even though I'm not usually afraid of doing that. The sheer variety of experience and skillsets ensures there is always an informed discussion. JOIN NOW!!

- **Jon Dews**, HR & Business Partner, Majestic 12 Ltd

If you are looking for a steady stream of thorough, pragmatic, and easily-digestible employment law advice, the HR Inner Circle is a great place to be.

- **Susi O'Brien**, Senior Manager HR, The Action Group

The regular updates are invaluable to not only me, but also my team. We find that they are presented in an easy to digest format and aren't too 'legalistic'.

- **Donna Negus**, Sekoya Specialist Employment Services

WWW.HRINNERCIRCLE.CO.UK

There aren't many other employment law advice services where you get direct access to an employment law barrister at a realistic price. Join the HR Inner Circle now – you won't regret it.

- **Kirsten Cluer**, Owner of Cluer HR, HR Consultancy

I like being able to use the HR Inner Circle Facebook group to ask other members for a second opinion, or for ideas when I get stuck with solving a tricky situation. There's usually someone who has come across the situation before.

- **Helen Astill**, Managing Director, Cherington HR Ltd

When I transitioned from big employers to an SME, I didn't realise how much I would miss having peers to kick ideas around. If you haven't got an internal network, you've got to build an external one. I got so much out of the discussion at an Inner Circle meetup recently and I look forward to getting the Inner Circular.

- **Elizabeth Divver**, Group HR Director, The Big Issue Group

Sign now! The monthly Q & A sessions are invaluable, the magazine is packed full of helpful info, you get lots of goodies and the Facebook page is really informative and a useful sounding board.

- **Caroline Hitchen**, Consultant, Caroline Neal Employment Law

WWW.HRINNERCIRCLE.CO.UK

Being a member of HR Inner Circle is one of the best sources of HR information and advice, and receiving the monthly audio seminars and magazines is extremely helpful and interesting. I can't recommend becoming a member highly enough. There is a private Facebook group which is great for asking other members advice and sharing knowledge and experiences. I have also recently attended one of the meetups that is organised by Daniel Barnett, and it was good to meet other members (and of course Daniel) in a more social setting. It was also a good opportunity to ask any questions you wanted and being able to get advice or support as to how they would deal with whatever you ask.

- **Tracey Seymour**, HR Manager (Head of Dept), Kumon Europe & Africa Ltd

---

The help and advice from other HR professionals on Facebook is really valuable, and quick. All the team enjoy the audio seminars and magazines for updates on current issues.

- **Catherine Larke**, Director | myHRdept.co.uk

WWW.HRINNERCIRCLE.CO.UK

For me it's a no brainer. We have a lot of really good contributors in the HR Inner Circle and it's more than a discussion forum and invaluable source of information. When combined with the magazine, the audio seminars and events, it is a complete service especially with Daniel's legal expertise always on hand.

- **Elizabeth Ince**, Self employed HR Consultant

Just join! It is invaluable with the resources you have at hand by joining the HR Inner Circle. Especially the Facebook Group where you can get advice or a different point of view that you may not have previously considered, outside of normal working hours which is very useful. Live Q&A's too.

- **Diana Wilks**, HR Manager, Go South Coast Ltd

HR can be complex because each and every issue will have its own set of individual circumstances. Being in the HR Inner Circle enables you to bounce ideas around and make sure you are considering every angle and aspect, knowing your HR Inner Circle partners will have had a similar experience to share.

- **Pam Rogerson**, HR Director, ELAS Group